Unruffled Roses

Connecting to Yourself, Resting your mind, and Other Intentional Self-care Tips

Dr. Celine Peace

Cover Designer: Monica Abraham

Interior Designer: Martinez Larry

Editorial: Bowler Henry

Unruffled Roses seems to be one of the most instructive and enlightening materials I am yet to read in a long time. The bespoke approach that Dr. Celine Peace gives to each of the chapters makes making a holistic self-care statement for the individual look like a walk in the park.

- **Prof. Catherine Puma** – one-time Counseling Psychologist with the American Psychological Association and editor to numerous self-care books.

The depth and analysis with which *Unruffled Roses* is written makes it a wonderful reading experience. This piece of self-care material clearly leads one in the path of goodness.

- **Marcus Braithwaite** – Senior Physiotherapist at the State Hospital, Johannesburg, South Africa

For the umpteenth time, we are yet remembered how our health, mind and daily living are much more important to us. Dr. Celine lights a candle to our path urging us to use wisdom in ensuring we look after ourselves. To me, *Unruffled Roses* is all but a glaring personification of the guided human who chooses to care for themself in a rather overworked world. I am definitely going to read this over and again.

- **Davies Martin, PhD** – Former Board Advisor for *the British Heart Foundation*, London, United Kingdom.

Contents

Unruffled Roses

Introduction

Moss roses are famed as one of the rarest breeds of Rose flowers that are as interesting as they are endearing. Also known as Purslane, the flower is so naturally fortified so much that it sustains itself at all seasons. During the summer dog days, the moss rose is well-known to survive taking advantage of its uniquely succulent leaves and brilliant blossoms. The garden plant gets to only about eight inches in height and spreads close to 20 inches which makes it a good ground cover or a supplement to a hanging basket.

The tissue paper-like petals close at night, creating colorful ground covers. Being a hardy annual flower that can absorb some cold weather, so it would not be destroyed by a light frost, the flower blooms well into the fall. Since I learned about the moss rose flowers many years back, I have not hesitated to plant them in my garden each succeeding year. Now, this is not a campaign for a neighborhood plantation of the beautiful garden plant. But beyond the abstract descriptives of a beautiful flower breed known as the moss rose, it is interesting for us to also take a cue from the refreshing candor that the moss rose flower affords us all. We all are like flowers. Thing is that not all flowers are good for a garden since some stand strong weathering the harsh seasons while many others fail to. Indeed, most garden lovers have always had to hire the services of horticulturists to recommend the best types that they could have within their gardens. And certain others have come to stumble on some other flower breeds and put them within the garden on their own without budging about whatever is there to know about those flowers.

The result is that a majority of the latter group end up needing to do a whole lot of work to keep and tend the plants. That whole BS could have been rightly avoided should they handpick just the suitable ones. In talking to horticulturists, I was made to realize how much valuable and self-sustaining the moss roses are amongst many others. For this cause, most garden lovers continue to be big fans of good-looking flowers. The moss rose did not just attract this to itself with a flash in the pan; the plant did make itself befitting of the gardener's choice due to its 'intentional' tendencies to care for itself regardless of the times. The point here is that we all become the best we can be when we learn to practice some self-care. The gardeners and of course, myself, would only like to have moss roses in my backdoor garden because it sustains itself thus straining me less while affording me the glorious scenery I want in a garden. And interestingly, this singular situation has greatly inspired this work.

Working as a therapist, I have encountered a huge number of people who continue to confess how much they could hardly bring themselves together due to the hurried lives they have chosen for themselves. As fascinating as it is to learn of how much they seem to have achieved for themselves in business and career, it does not translate into so much fulfillment and joy for them. I have attended to multi-millionaires who admitted how wretched they feel despite the castles they have built for themselves in the business world over time. Unluckily, they are not okay with their situations. On a serious note, I have witnessed about a hundred who have confided in me how much they feel they could do better if they were to start from the ground up again – they made it clear outright that they would choose to tend after themselves than they did in pursuit of what they apparently felt would make them feel happy but never did.

The resounding word on my lips every occasion I have the opportunity to talk to people – individually and collectively - about how important they need to see themselves is self-care. To remain unruffled like the moss rose whether in winter or summer demands that individuals make a solid self-care statement that befits their psyche and fulfillment. We need to make up our minds to count the fine art of connecting to ourselves and resting our minds as important as tending to our businesses and careers. It is high time humans stopped seeing the choice of what makes them genuinely happy and content as not selfishness in the real sense. Rather, self-care it is. In a world filled with so much disquiet, amplified by the false connections that technology shoves down our throats, we must choose to be concerned about doing what suits us best – our health, families, and mind. With every episode I get to water my moss roses I am constantly reminded of the need to look after myself as well. As an aside, as bemoaning as most social security advocates may insist the institutions have a huge role to play, while agreeing to this, I strongly feel putting the best foot forward comes with a firm individual decision to practice self-care in every possible sense of it. For if we do not care for ourselves, who will?

This book contains seemingly disjointed yet holistically connected thoughts, ideas, and research efforts geared toward ensuring you get the best when it comes to practicing self-care.

The first three chapters clearly capture how we met ourselves where we are. Hurried speed clamped together with the rise in mental and physical stress and the bane in technology are all responsible for the debilitating situations of exhaustion and ill-health humankind experiences. The next chapter underlines an instructive note that brings together the tell-tale signs of taking life too seriously. This part seems to be the springboard for the introduction of the workable approaches that self-care would consist of as identified in the remaining chapters. The remaining five chapters include themes on mindfulness, healthier meals, less stress and focused speed, music and reading, and a handful of helpful hints on self-care. Each of these chapters, no doubt, enlighten, inform and remind us how we can cultivate the beautiful art of self-care such that we as moss roses can stay unruffled all day all time.

CHAPTER ONE:

TRACING IT BACK TO HURRIED SPEED

These days, we work faster, drive faster, communicate faster, and eat faster - to put it plainly, we live so, so fast. The time reserve we have courtesy of tech has been counterbalanced by the increase in complicatedness, decisions, interferences, assumptions, stress, deferrals, and blunders. But our bodies are not meant to work at hurried speed and we are confronted with different illnesses to the point that "recovering" has turned into some other time shopper.

Interestingly, this chapter readily appraises the art of discouraging hurried speed and not just 'speed'. Speed is good. It revolves around every significant progress in human living. The ascent towards all notable milestones set in human history has been one way or the other earmarked by speed. However, when speed becomes hurried, it is not out of place to raise a question mark. We need to ask ourselves how much this is beneficial to everything that is as equally as important to human life as these other areas which provoke hurried speed. When our perceived speed comes at the very expense of peace, health, and relationships, we must be proactive enough to apply the brakes. Here we are talking about how much of a sound mind, good health, and human connection we can enjoy while on speed under the guise of treading the path of progress.

Our everyday routine is being carried out at a lot quicker pace than quite it is half a century ago - or even quite a few decades back. We have so much affective love for speed. And it extends over to the ludicrous. From cheap food and momentary downloads to one-minute sleep time stories and drive-through memorial services, organizations are striving to get our limited time.

The typical business lunch is down to 30 minutes or less. A recent article asserts the typical jobber eats their lunch within minutes.

The saying "lunch hour" is a misnomer. Everybody appears to be resolved to pressing increasingly more into each hour, some, in any event, munching fast food as they run through their email(s). In the same article, written by Wigglesworth Baron, you can find out about what speed means for how we work and live.

The Perils of Hurried Speed

Over and beyond, we are forsaking rest and available time. The typical American presently gets an hour and a half less rest a night than they did a hundred years back. Yet, the sluggishness that results from catching less than a normal amount of sleep causes more fender benders than liquor. In the course of my life, I have come to discover that the typical measure of rest we get has diminished from a little more than 8 hours out of every night to barely 5 hours. Getting less than 5 hours of rest a night can impede the coordination of our human engine, discourse, reflexes, and judgment.

What speed means for our wellbeing

Since we don't make time to eat appropriately, practice, or rest

adequately, we gain more body weight. It is commonly accepted

that that has become a scourge in the U.S. Up to 33% of

Americans are clinically weighty. It's fascinating to take note that

youngsters in schools within strolling distance of drive-through

eateries will generally be obese. Around one-fifth of Canadians are

hefty. The circumstance is by all accounts better in the event that

we need to walk farther to get to our drive-through eateries.

When we take our walk faster, talk faster, work faster, talk quicker,

sleep less, and utilize tech more, there is no reason for our body

efficiency not to get through the rooftop and everything that has

been going on with all the extra relaxation time

We don't achieve more by doing it at a higher speed

I feel we achieve minimal more than we have consistently

achieved. We're simply doing it at a higher speed. The time saved

is being filled by interferences and low-impact activities. Sofia

Raleigh, in her book, The Fantasy of Multi-tasking notes that reviews show, by and large, every individual loses 28% of the normal business day because of interferences and failure. I have gleaned from comparative statistical reports, for example, that about 3 hours each day is wasted in interferences.

Technology has made us assume that performing multiple tasks saves time when the inverse is the case. Studies reveal that when we move about to and fro beginning with one errand and then onto the next, our minds' brain circuits get a little break in between - a tedious process that could lessen our effectiveness by half.

That's it "personal time"

In this high-speed clime, numerous conventional systems are losing their effect or just never again work. Calm hours, as we probably are aware of them, are a relic of days gone by. Schedules are losing their viability. Focus is getting powerless or non-existent. Performing multiple tasks has just become counterproductive.

Now and again, even setting objectives has become impossible. Eating on the go has turned into the standard. Rest, generally speaking, is viewed as an irritating need. We are investing more energy in getting more materialistic than in remaining healthy. Even the pretty thin line between work and individual life has become obscure. Discretionary time is vanishing. Stress and the absence of balance are usually connected with our evolving climate.

The detriments of technology

There are benefits presented by the innovation that tech brings with it yet there are also hindrances. Technology is erasing the already blurred lines between work and home. With PDAs and mobile phones, we can be reached whenever. Our daily agenda goes with us any place we go. So we must be self-guided to the point that we overlook emails and mute our cellphones.

It is similarly as vital to plan time with family, time alone, and recreation time just as it is to plan conferences, arrangements, and other business endeavors. We ought to be consistently inquiring as to whether the all-out time we are enjoying with our family and friends is in accordance with how much we esteem them.

There is a prevailing need beckoning at us to plan our work around our lives; not to plan our lives around our works. On the contrary, work might spread all through our whole day and gulp up our endeavors, putting our lives out of balance. The vast majority don't require help identifying their needs; they need help with living their needs.

CHAPTER TWO:

THE RISE IN MENTAL AND PHYSICAL STRESS

There is just an overwhelming amount of things we need to do and the details that are fast sweeping all over our psyche. Due to this, medical and psychological experts alike have discovered that the humans affected experience what is called notable depressive disorders (NDDs). Perhaps, this might sound like an alarming bell to everyone who chooses to cherry-pick the grit of the busy life over watching over their health.

More so, a disturbing new study reveals that individuals working over 56 hours weekly are at significant danger of dying from exhaustion. It's killing 75% of a million individuals every year.

Ryan Barton disregarded the major side effects. All things considered, the 49-year-old business analyst was an exceptionally dynamic, fit lover of veggies, who cycled much of the time and kept away from high-fat food varieties. He was a long way from the regular survivor of heart failure.

Notwithstanding, the LA-based Barton was working 58-hour long weeks of work, including nights and ends of the week. He was confronting tight deadlines and overseeing complex computerized projects. This responsibility was completely ordinary to him. "I have an extremely high-stress work… I'm always over-driven," he mutters.

It was only after a while before when he spontaneously began feeling an iron block-like tension on her chest, that he started to genuinely take her side effects more seriously. At the clinic, it became clear he had a tear in one of his arteries. This is a sign of a spontaneous coronary artery dissection (SCAD), a somewhat uncommon heart condition that especially affects ladies and individuals below age 50. Informed that he would require an angioplasty to open up the artery affected, Barton thought, "There is just no time for this. I've plans for movements at work, and I'm doing everything."

Like Barton, many are likewise confronting chronic illnesses because of the cutthroat arrangements for clearing their rack of work. Recent, sobering research - said to be the very first review to evaluate the worldwide impact of infection from working extended periods - has shown how disheartening the circumstance is.

In a paper put into circulation on 17 May, authors from establishments including the World Health Organization (WHO) and the International Labor Organization (ILO) propose that every year, 75% of a million individuals draw their last breath due to ischemic coronary illness and stroke, because of working extended periods. (Ischemic coronary illness, otherwise called coronary heart illness, includes narrowed routes. Barton's SCAD is not the same as traditional ischemic coronary illness, yet stress and hypertension are central to both.)

At the end of the day, a bigger number of individuals are passing on from exhaustion than they do from malaria. This is a worldwide health emergency, demanding consideration from people, organizations, and states all the same. Curiously, in case we don't tackle it, the issue may not just proceed - it could deteriorate.

What exhaustion means for health

In the paper, published in the journal Climate Global, specialists methodically looked into information on lengthy working hours, characterized as 56 hours or more each week; health effects; and death rates from the vast majority of the world's nations, from 2000 to 2019. The authors controlled for factors such as financial status and gender, to establish the unadulterated impacts of overwork on health.

The review lays out that overwork remains the single biggest risk factor for work-related illness, representing about 33% of the burden of sickness connected with work. "For me, as a disease transmission specialist, I was very shocked when we did the math," remarks Cardozo Percy, a WHO technical official and the lead author of the paper. "I was very shocked by the size of the weight." He depicts the discoveries as moderate, yet at the same clinically critical.

There are two significant ways that overwork can lessen health and life span. One is the biological cost of persistent pressure, with an increase in stress hormones resulting in heightened pulse and cholesterol. Then there are the progressions in behavior. Those logging in for extended periods might be resting pretty little, scarcely working out, eating improper food varieties, and smoking and drinking to adapt.

Furthermore, there are specific reasons to worry about exhaustion both while we're still in the Coronavirus pandemic, and having a look at life from that point. The pandemic has increased some work stresses while bringing new types of workplace weariness.

India has turned into the focal point of the worldwide pandemic, with extra 25 million cases of Coronavirus. Yet, the pandemic is affecting health in alternate ways also. Carlos Sijh, a doctor and a pioneering member of the Indian Heart Association, points out that South Asians are as of now at high risk of coronary illness. Presently, "with the Coronavirus pandemic we have seen an expansion in virtual work, which has obscured the balance of work and life among numerous people, resulting in disturbed sleep patterns and exercise; this has thus heightened the risk for cardiovascular illness and stroke."

Besides, the pandemic has brought about the most awful financial slump since the Great Depression. Past economic downturns have really been trailed by the increase in working hours. "It seems to be practically similar to an unreasonable impact," Carlos identifies, considering the widespread employment setbacks while a recession continues. However, "the truth is by all accounts that individuals who are as yet working need to work more to make up for the employment setbacks."

Major Points of Overwork

As per the information in the paper, 9% of the total populace - a number that incorporates youngsters - is working for extended periods. What's more, starting around 2000, the quantity of exhausting individuals has been expanding.

Overwork impacts various groups of workers in totally different ways.

Men work longer hours than ladies in each age circle. Overwork tops in early middle age, albeit the health impacts take more time to turn up. (The review authors utilized a 10-year slack period to follow the impacts of overwork at the start of any sickness; all things considered, "death by overwork" doesn't work out just that simple.)

As indicated by the new information, burning the midnight candles and extended periods is presently not just debilitating - it's life suffocating

The data likewise shows that individuals in Southeast Asia appear to be working the longest hours; individuals in Europe, the briefest. Carlos sheds light further that there might be social purposes behind the bigger extent of individuals in Asia working for extended periods. Also, many individuals work in the informal sector in low- and mid-income Asian nations. As Carlos references, "Individuals in the informal economy could need to work extended periods to get by, they may be maintaining numerous sources of income, they probably won't be covered by social security regulations."

On the other side, numerous Europeans partake in an organized society that celebrates lengthy holidays and significant rest periods. This more relaxed mien is backed by the law; for example, the European Association's Working Time Directive bars representatives from working over forty-eight hours weekly by and large.

Be that as it may, even in a few European nations, particularly aside from France and Scandinavia, there's been a rising proportion of highly-talented specialists working a higher number of hours beginning around 1990 (after the pinnacle of unionization and the connected representative securities). Obviously, the Austrian health minister left his work in April, saying that he had grown hypertension and high glucose while being a workaholic during the pandemic. His public declaration was uncommon as a result of his high-profile position, yet also since he was really ready to leave his debilitating job.

Over in Washington, Barton has likewise been lucky, in that his partners have supported her need to relax her work. Since not every individual can cope with working more adjusted hours, and not every person will get a reminder before a lethal stroke or respiratory failure, there's a dire need to handle this health emergency now.

Confronting Overwork

If these ugly patterns go on in the same way, overwork - and the related health danger - will just increase. This is particularly stressing, considering the number of societies that celebrate overwork to the point of burnout. Also, as our work hours have ticked up during the pandemic, with few indications of halting, those who spend an excessive number of hours on the clock will just increase.

The need to interrupt the cycle falls on both managers and employees somehow - and all might have to cooperate to assume control over overwork and the ensuing issues that follow.

Those logging extended periods might be resting pretty little, hardly working out, eating unsavory food varieties, and smoking and drinking to adapt

By and large, Carlos urges workplaces to embrace adaptable work, work sharing, and different methods for further enhancing balance in work arrangements. They ought to likewise treat work-related health administrations seriously. What's more, Carlos remarks,

"We at the Indian Heart Association accept that increased training and screening is vital to forestall cardiovascular illness and stroke."

There's a job for individual workers to reshape their mentalities to fill in too - we can all attempt to stand up against the draw of overwork that keeps so many of us stuck to our Cellphones until quite a bit later. The sooner workers do this, the better position they'll be in; since overwork remains a risk that accumulates over the years, keeping it from becoming persistent may diminish the seriousness of the most horrendously terrible health risks.

Yet, the most far-reaching developments would have to happen at the legislative level. According to Carlos, "We already have plans. Individuals have set up limits on the highest number of hours we ought to work" - for example, with the European Working Time Directive, or other right-to-detach regulations. In nations with firm regulations on work restrictions, what's key is upholding and observing those regulations. Also, in nations with infirm social security nets, anti-poverty measures and government welfare projects can bring down the number of individuals exhausting themselves to the extreme to make both ends meet.

In the final analysis, the issue of overwork - and the medical implication it breeds - will continue in case we do not make changes in our working lives. What's more, change isn't unthinkable. "We can follow through with something," insists Carlos. "This is for everybody."

CHAPTER THREE:

THE BANE OF TECHNOLOGY ON HUMAN FOCUS

I am poised to contend that we are presently experiencing the transition from the Data Age to what I call the Time of Retribution.

In the Modern Age and the Data Age, there was this broad idealism that technology would ultimately take care of our concerns in general — destitution, illness, brutality, and others. Over the most recent 5 years or thereabouts, it's been gradually occurring to us that more and more technology, without help from anyone else, can't be the way out, and, the arrangements that we have put in place at present, while they tackle a few issues, make different issues that might be similarly extreme.

While technology or innovation has positively lifted numerous people out of neediness and improved our lives in numerous ways, it has additionally made the world progressively mind-boggling and challenging to explore. The fast disturbance of many laid-out ventures has implied that even the wisest and upright people have needed to struggle to remain relevant in the advanced globalized economy — while others, immersed with information to get a handle on, can't sort out some way to settle on the appropriate choices the initial time, and should go through years broke, jobless, underemployed, or worn out. We are not more fragile or dumber than our predecessors, however the world is more difficult than any other time in recent times and we want to go through more experimentation than they did to get a familiar presence.

Technological advancement will flourish material increase considerably more, yet technological innovation alone can't tackle the issue of sorting out whom to convey resources to and getting everybody energetic about how resources are appropriated.

The web has empowered new methods of social collaboration that the development of our normal minds didn't prepare us to deal with. Despite the way that we should be more connected than any other time in recent times, many individuals are desolate and kept from veritable positive human connection. Many individuals don't have a place with "communities" or "groups" in which people are esteemed, how our predecessors have had for centuries; all things considered, we as a whole seek attention on a globalized market afforded by social channels, and many individuals are losing the opposition, becoming desolate and discouraged, while even the individuals who are winning, getting a bigger portion of the seeming positive attention than others, can frequently be restless and uncertain about keeping up with their situation in the present progressive system, since they, as well, frequently come up short on affectionate get-togethers in which individuals really care about them.

Monetary development and innovative improvement don't build the proportion of accessible human consideration regarding how much is needed for human connection (as both scale directly with the number of people alive). We need to concede that we just don't have the foggiest idea about how to take care of this issue at present, yet anyway, clear that we can't depend on technology to be our savior.

I trust that to defy the serious issues that we will confront for a hundred years, we must search internally and stand up to a few awkward insights about human instinct, comprehend the way that innovation can enhance both the best and the most obviously terrible parts of it, and perhaps meet up to make huge commitments to create a world that is better for us all.

Contemporary technology remains a perfect representation of the innate capability of the human psyche. We are living in a period of hyper-network and fast-paced production.

It is intriguing to reach out to a friend or family member across the globe, shop on the web and get the request conveyed to one's doorstep shortly, purchase food or fast food quickly, and get quick approvals via social channels.

The Coronavirus pandemic has simply added to the ease of doing nearly everything on the web -, for example, school classes, work gatherings, business coordinated efforts, health meetings, banking, shopping, and a lot more.

In any case, to whom much is given, much will be expected. Could it be said that we are utilizing innovation or would we say we are being utilized? This is food for thought for every single one of us to exclusively consider.

The Effect on Human Health

Each tool that has benefits likewise has its limitations. While innovation has made metropolitan life helpful and cooperative, it is at the expense of computerized addiction, psychological wellness problems, eye conditions, postural irregularities, and a large group of different infections.

From a Yogic point of view, a lot of openness to electronic gadgets inconveniently affects our prosperity. Shobhit Raj carefully notes in an expository essay that the electromagnetic radiation transmitted from these devices brings down Prana, the indispensable life force inside, and imbalances the Vata Dosha, which prompts uneasiness, and fretfulness, a sleeping disorder, and other anxious lopsided characteristics.

Yet, the harm likewise happens mentally, as the substance we consume can change our belief system. At the point when we are associated with cynicism through the internet-based world, it shapes our considerations and sentiments at an unobtrusive level.

While any physical or mental well-being lopsidedness can be amended with all-encompassing health treatment, two angles require our attention the most - persistence and focus.

The Impact on the Psyche

Our capacity to focus has debased extensively throughout recent many years. Each age is an observer of the changing scene of how we consume data.

Perusing books might be an intriguing side-interest today with the wide access to book recordings, podcasts, and recordings on the web. To add to the digitization of information and amusement, we are likewise barraged with short-structure content.

This short-structure content comprises 30-second stories, 1-minute video reels, and the perpetual look via social network phases. This might appear to be a pretentious sign of the cerebrum's ability to deal with data and perform various tasks.

Be that as it may, truly, it is changing the compound arrangement of the cerebrum. This plan of short-structure content makes it habit-forming and a person continues to surf info via litanies of social media handles to look for a dopamine hit of eccentricity and energy.

Adding to this, there is likewise the choice to go through longer content at twice the typical speed. We are all in a test of skill and endurance, urgently bouncing from one action then onto the next, that we are fooled into feeling useful.

Be that as it may, this consumption pattern of twice the speed and short-structure content makes one anxious in genuine situations, outside the hi-tech bubble. This is obvious in individuals not having the persistence to pay attention to others and intruding on others with their perspective.

It additionally means us anticipating that things should happen immediately because the advanced world works that way. However, obviously, this present reality is totally different. All that requires some commitment and we need to develop persistence with external frameworks and cycles throughout daily life.

With this sort of consumption pattern on the web, envision the effect on our power to focus. Youngsters are experiencing their childhood in this universe of data glut and interruption, and they are negatively impacted the most.

Grown-ups too are succumbing to this snare of advanced traps, and this is appearing in individuals losing interest in work, being confounded about their motivation, and having an unending barrage of thoughts on their minds.

In each area of life, be it business, connections, or creativity, and spiritual growth - the main apparatus is focus. An engaged brain doesn't lose track and is a proficient war kit to confront all interruptions of alarms, new information, news, and other commotion on the web.

There is positively a beam of hope. We are honored with an inborn gift called mindfulness, which can assist with acknowledging disastrous patterns and rework the brain to change our relationship with technological innovation.

A Reasonable Aid

In the event that we see data as nourishment for the psyche, we will understand the harm of "voraciously consuming food". The vast majority eat a few dinners every day. Assuming we eat without break, and numerous dinners over the course of the day, we will wind up with some imbalance and sickness in the body.

Likewise, consuming data online ceaselessly without breaks and a goal in focus will provoke mental blockage or runs, and manifest as uneasiness, wretchedness, and other mental uneven characters.

Here are a few hints to developing a sound and healthy relationship with technology:

❖ Try not to really look at your telephone for the first several hours in the first section of the day. Begin your morning schedule with yourself, and not the outside world.

❖ Keep notifications OFF while working, to stay away from interruptions. It is useful to focus on and center on the movement or task within reach.

- ❖ Check your telephone just at explicit spans during the day. (E.g. after breakfast, after lunch, before supper). Seriously, we CAN live without our cellphones.

- ❖ Track the time spent on your telephone on an everyday or weekly basis. This will assist with grasping your level of consumption. Numerous apps have a component to follow consumption designs.

- ❖ Switch off all electronic devices basically an hour prior to bed. This will likewise work with a more profound and peaceful rest.

- ❖ Be conscious of your feelings while using the web. Web-based entertainment can provoke fundamental jealousy, desire, outrage, dread, frailty, responsibility, pride, and different feelings.

- ❖ Try not to practice it all the time to involve technology as a refrain from awkward circumstances and horrendous feelings. Diversion is a piece of present-day life, yet need not be the characterizing element of our lives.

❖ Consume content that summons sensations of idealism, as opposed to suffocating in cynicism and misleading publicity. All information feeds the mind.

❖ Practice digital abstinence consistently. For example, detach from your cellphone on a Sunday, or don't surf social networks for a week. These occasional regimens will assist with resetting the cerebrum and make space for internal awareness.

Something to think about

The "smart" phone is intended to complement our innate knowledge and make our lives more brilliant, instead of making us data-age slaves who succumb to tech carelessly.

This is vital in the event that one is stepping the yogic way. All that we consume with our faculties have an enduring effect on the unpretentious layers of the psyche. These impressions, noted as Samskaras, over the long run are well established and impact our considerations, feelings, convictions, propensities, and way of life.

Likewise, one of the greatest perspectives according to Yoga, is Ekagrata, a one-pointed centered mind. As stressed before, this perspective will assist us with conquering tangible interruptions and continue to walk forward toward the ultimate objective of any pursuit.

All in all, to address the question raised hitherto - Would we say we are utilizing technological innovation or would we say we are being utilized?

The response is somehow, however, I accept that the last option is the prompter reality with regards to our shared awareness. Be that as it may, we in all actuality do have independence, and pursuing careful decisions will act as a powerful safeguard against the impediments of technology.

According to Frank Hebert, "Innovation is both an instrument for aiding people and for obliterating them. This is the irony of our times which we are constrained to confront"

The tech boom is an amazing asset, yet the critical lies in the way we coordinate it into our high-speed metropolitan lives. We can either surrender to the data glut, or we can utilize constant attention to recollect that there is a lovely world past these devices.

Check around you and connect to yourself, and be close to nature. Hold in high esteem the present sky, the present earth, the present trees, the present, delightful blossoms, and the present lively birds and creatures.

Get back to reading nurturing books, palpate the surface of every page, and be part of the quietness which goes with you and the book.

Relish your dinner alone or with friends and family contented, detached from all interruptions. Keep your telephone to the side while with another person. Offer them your complete attention as opposed to subliminally expecting the oncoming tweet.

Digital fillings won't ever impact our minds in the manner in which nature and association with others cause us to feel. Attempt it yourself for a day! Disengage from your cellphone and PC to reconnect with the delight and endowments throughout everyday life.

Change begins from the inside. May we as a whole be motivated toward building a delightful reality where we are companions with tech, instead of being constrained by it? For in the latter event, it becomes a bane!

CHAPTER FOUR:

NOT GETTING OUT OF LIFE ALIVE: WHEN TOO MUCH IS TOO MUCH

A staggering number of us take ourselves too seriously, and that shows how much pressure we have on our regular routines. Imagine a scenario where we ventured back for a couple of moments to recall that there's something else to life besides our work titles, wads of cash, achievements, degrees, and whatever else we relate to. The majority of us invest such a lot of energy attempting to become something and beat deterrents and excel that we neglect to just breathe, chuckle, and take in the magnificence that encompasses us consistently. We let the voices in our minds let us know we aren't sufficient way time after time, and we begin to trust them sooner or later.

Life doesn't need to feel like a steady fight; you can decide to have a more happy approach, and simply ride on the influxes of life as opposed to struggling to stay above water.

Van Wilder captures the point here more succinctly: "Don't take life seriously; nobody ever makes it out alive anyway."

The following are some of the signs you are spreading yourself too thin:

❖ **You could hardly recall the last time you laughed at yourself - or anything by any means, besides.**

Several kinds of research have been established in the previous ten years in regards to the extraordinary medical advantages of laughing, and how it truly is the best medication. Chuckling has been demonstrated to lessen pressure, battle tension, and despondency, further develop memory, lower pulse, and pulse, discharge endorphins into the body, and even accentuate oxygen levels to various body organs. It offers plenty of medical advantages, and in particular, it helps you not treat life as such in a serious way.

In the event that you don't recollect the last time you laughed, I would suggest taking the most noteworthy measures of laughter that you can, because keeping our hearts light cheerfully permit us to carry on with a better, more extravagant life.

Go out with companions, watch an interesting YouTube video, or do anything that puts a grin on your face. That you have the stuff to attend to throughout your everyday life doesn't mean you can't live your life up even so!

❖ **You believe you must protect yourself continually.**

In the event that you go over the top with yourself, you will probably feel like everybody is going after you and trying to get under your skin. You could see the world as a threatening, unpleasant spot, in which you should safeguard your space and convictions. Nonetheless, having this demeanor will just hold people back from drawing near to you, and won't help you with getting much less on your plate. The vast majority on the planet really love contacting others and having clever discussions without wanting to destruct or go after others for their convictions or character.

Assuming you feel compromised by others, work on your levels of confidence with the goal that others begin to seem to be companions as opposed to adversaries in your eyes.

- ❖ **You get annoyed when others question your convictions.**

As an elaboration of the last point, you shouldn't feel compromised or tense when others pose inquiries about your convictions or perspectives. You ought to have the option to have a socialized, open discussion with somebody without taking it to the limit and feeling like you should become protective about it. If you don't like to explain the way you feel about an idea, you don't need to, yet more often than not, others simply need to get to know you and have only good intentions.

Try not to over-commit to your convictions; rather, keep a receptive outlook so you can learn a lesson from others, and they may very well take a moral from you, too.

❖ **You constantly need some goal to pursue to be cheerful.**

People are goal-prone entities naturally. We need to have something to focus on, something to pursue, and something to achieve. Having a fantasy and pursuing it is perfect, however not when it removes you from the present and keeps you from getting a charge out of life in the present. Since you have something you need to accomplish from here on out, doesn't mean you can't embrace the present. In the event that you can't feel blissful without having something to pursue continually, then you could learn that your 'too much' is becoming too much. Attempt to take part in the easily overlooked details about existence, and recollect the main thing: your family, companions, wellbeing, and how you treat others.

❖ **You contrast yourself with others ceaselessly.**

With social networks and different types of amusement and media sources, we don't need to look exceptionally far to track down somebody to contrast ourselves with. Be that as it may, this may make us unpleasant and critical eventually, and never really helpful to us with having a decent outlook on ourselves. Next time you discover yourself doing this, recollect that nobody can impersonate or imitate you. So go out there and show the world your interesting gifts and abilities, and quit attempting to become another person. You will just lose yourself by attempting to be somebody else, so go with the decision to adore yourself today. Should you quit viewing yourself so pretentiously and figure out how to unwind into your uniqueness, you will begin to have a more open, cherishing viewpoint about existence, and simply absorb the scenery while you can.

❖ You don't have a funny bone

Assuming that you lash out when somebody prods you, it could mean you're excessively intense. It's generally expected to get into amicable chats at work, home, or school. Assuming you get insulted when individuals do this, you're overall excessively intense. Obviously, there is an opportunity to be serious, however not constantly. Having a comical tendency is sound and encourages everyone around you.

Rather than taking yourself too seriously, unwind and let yourself jump in and let loose of the normal prodding. Friendly teasing is generally a sign that individuals feel good around you.

❖ You seem intense

If you make too much of yourself, you might feel it means quite a bit to seem to be extreme and solid. Maybe you feel this a lot that you consider it hard to be open to individuals. Being solid is something you take cover behind to avoid others at all costs.

Assuming this is you; make sure to show up not exactly as solid, particularly around reliable loved ones. Keep in mind; that it's OK to act naturally, not an extreme facade to take cover behind.

❖ You do not forgive yourself

One sign that you're excessively intense is that you are too unforgiving with yourself. You feel like you want to work harder than every other person. You might challenge yourself and choke up your timetable. Similarly, you believe you want to accomplish other things than others to feel far better about yourself.

If you feel like this, it very well might be instructive to step back and assess why you're doing this. Perhaps you feel deficient, so you're attempting to show what you can do. Give yourself some space and unwind.

❖ Lash out when you commit errors

Demeaning reflections over simple errors are normal if you take your life too seriously. Everybody has their faults. Regardless of whether your missteps appear to be huge from the get-go, they presumably aren't quite as critical as you suspect. The vast majority don't for even a moment notice others' errors. Being your most awful critic is an easy ditch to fall into. Be careful!

At the point when you commit an error, make an effort not to treat it so in a serious way. Find a lesson you can draw from your error, and resolve to give it a try once more.

❖ **You attempt to control everything**

There are numerous things in life that you just have no control over. Being excessively wary and controlling is a certain sign you're excessively serious about life. Obviously, there are numerous things in life you can and ought to control, yet you want to give up and trust God to assist you with those things that are beyond your control.

Being an obsessive-compulsive person is debilitating and it won't ever work. Something in life will be beyond your control. Attempt to relinquish your feelings of trepidation and longing to assume control. Seek God for help and entrust him with those wild affairs you encounter. The common peacefulness prayer communicates this thought this way:

"God, afford me the tranquility to acknowledge the things I can't change, the fortitude to change the things I can, and the insight to get the difference."

❖ **Everything revolves around you**

At the point when you take life too seriously, you just can't relinquish your ego. Everything is about you and how it affects you or your look. You might relate to this by:

- Staying away from social circumstances where you feel really awkward

- Excessively agonizing over others' opinions of you

- Flying off the handle where somebody doesn't offer you the consideration you assume you merit

- Expecting individuals ought to understand what you want, so you don't inquire

- Moving discussions back to yourself as opposed to zeroing in on the other individual

- Attempt to step back and harness your ego. Expect that you're not the main individual in the room and focus on others.

❖ **You're not modest**

When too much is too much for you usually implies you could do without being told you're in the wrong. Perhaps you could do without getting criticized at work. Modesty is having a low assessment of your indispensability. And as serious as it may prove, being indispensable anywhere is more probably Utopian.

Notable Characteristics of modesty include:

- Being appreciative

- Not flaunting yourself or your achievements

- Not surrendering to pride or self-importance

- Being benevolent; not inconsiderate

- Not disparaging others

Start practicing these little things in your day-to-day existence. Prefer to be lowly when you're enticed to be prideful. Continue to work at it. You can develop your traits of modesty as you practice them consistently.

❖ You're a maverick

Individuals who rock and roll with loved ones are more joyful and livelier than those who decide to be separated from everyone else. They commonly live longer than those who are less associated with their community. It's OK to be separated from everyone else some of the time, however, if you pull away from individuals constantly, it's not the best. Identify ways of engaging with a healthy community of like minds. Endeavor to quit taking yourself rather seriously and let others into your reality.

❖ You can't offer commendations

Assuming you're excessively serious, you might think that offering compliments are deceitful. Or then again maybe you see no good thing in others to commend. Both of these considerations imply your ego is having a field day. Offering praises is basically dead on assuming your intention is to energize somebody, not simply compliment them. Watch out for good things that others do and truly praise them about it.

❖ You're not appreciative

Research reveals that gratitude and prosperity are forever inseparable. Individuals who offer thanks more often are more joyful. They consider themselves consistently as being a gift from God. They don't underestimate things or individuals. Thankfulness is a way out of being excessively serious. Cultivating positivity assists you with appreciating life. You're not as up to speed in finding success, yet be a part of the experience of being alive.

In case you carry yourself too seriously, it very well might be an ideal opportunity to glance around at every one of the good things you have in your daily life. Regardless of whether you are challenged in life, there is continuously a person or thing in your life you can be thankful for.

Final Reflections

Living, all by itself, is a struggle. It's easy to get preoccupied with getting along with work, companions, and family. A lot of pressure in your life will make you excessively intense. Assuming you end your life too severely, it could be an ideal opportunity to step forward and reconsider your life. Attempt to incorporate appreciation, giggling, and praising others in your day. Take a good bite of your life's pie, even with every one of the shortcomings. There is magnificence surrounding you should you require some effort to see it. Today is a decent day to quit taking life too seriously and appreciate being what your identity was meant to be.

CHAPTER FIVE:

MINDFULNESS TO THE RESCUE: HINTS FOR HELP

As an always-busy full-time jobber, life can get exceptionally chaotic. Countless times I would get back home from work unable to unwind owing to the persistent pressure from the day's work. Thinking about forthcoming activities and approaching deadlines in every case always leave me tensed up.

My family life was beginning to go through a lot as I was unable to get myself together; I felt restless and immediately got baffled over the most minor issues.

Then I found out about mindfulness-oriented stress reduction.

The good news is that practicing mindfulness day by day has completely changed my life. I feel okay and more conscious of how I'm feeling. Also, I can communicate my thoughts better, take care of issues that emerge with added grit, and become more present.

You can improve your life as well.

What's the hue and cry over mindfulness, anyway?

Although mindfulness proposes that the mind is completely aware of what circumvents you, it is way more than that. At the very root of mindfulness, we can be right now and have a total consciousness of our body, our location, and what's going on around us without being responsive.

Care easily falls into place for us; however, a few methods permit us to rehearse it alongside reflection to accomplish a complete state of relaxation.

What Is Reflection?

Reflection is all about preparing your body through different methods to zero in on the present time. Also known as meditation, reflection remains a method for assisting you with acquiring a sound viewpoint on what is happening in your life by helping you with tuning in completely to your viewpoints and feelings to grasp them.

Health with Mindfulness

Mindfulness is something other than managing stress. It is the hyper-ready attention to how you are feeling and what is happening in your life. There are a few advantages that are upheld through assessments and underline the varying advantages that practicing mindfulness affords you.

Practicing mindfulness with meditation gives you the advantage of decreasing directionless thinking. This means you will be less bothered about something specific and more inclined towards everything in all.

You will want to support your memory to assist you in reviewing things effortlessly. You will never again be as fretted over where your motor keys are or the relevant cutoff time you have coming up.

Enhance your focus so you can concentrate without being diverted by different things happening around you. As a bustling professional, this assisted me with zeroing in on the snapshot of being with family as opposed to all the stuff from work that was overloading my psyche.

Through mindfulness coupled with meditation, you will encounter a lift in those expressive energies. Issues that you struggle to deal with will have an answer as you can concoct more smart ways to settle them.

Beginning with Mindfulness

At the point when you are simply beginning, mindfulness with meditation can very well prove to be awkward. The justification for the awkward inclination is that you are retraining your mind.

The initial period of beginning for me was the hardest. Be that as it may, it comes all the more normally after some time.

> You need not distract yourself with any special tools or paid-for sessions to practice the art of mindfulness.

> Sit down. You can either use a seat or the floor - whichever works for you.

> Focus on your legs. They are either straight before you, crossed under you, or just resting from your situated position.

> You need to fix your chest area. Try not to harden your back; you may feel awkward if you do so. Rather, fix your chest area into a decent stance that feels normal.

> You would like for your upper arms to be lined up with your chest area.

> Then, drop your jaw a bit. You would like for your look to fall low tenderly without feeling constrained.

> Put your focus on the moment you are dropping your jaw. Stay there for a couple of moments and be at that time.

> Breathe and feel it when you do. Try not to force your breath or attempt to heighten it at any rate; feel your breath in its normal state.

> Try not to overreact assuming that your mind begins to stray from the relaxation process. It is unavoidable that your attention will float from your breath to other things.

> Take a moment before you change any actual position. Regardless of whether you shift your legs a bit, try stopping first.

> Try not to stress over the way that your mind will meander. Expect that your mind meandering will happen continually.

> At the point when you feel prepared or loose, delicately lift your eyes. Assuming you were rehearsing mindfulness with your eyes closed, open them.

Step-by-step Guidelines to Practice Mindfulness and Reflection

As you dismiss your mind from the normal things that mess with your mind and focus on what your body does, you are practicing mindfulness and reflection. Nonetheless, that is far from simple or easy. There are a couple of ways you can practice mindfulness and reflection in a viable manner.

Mindfulness in regular day-to-day Living

There are ways you can practice mindfulness-based stress reduction while approaching your daily work.

You can learn to focus on what your body does while you take a walk. You focus on the thing you're doing as you get on. Mind the purposes of your actions. Lace your shoes with intent, and focus on the thing you are doing as you are making it happen.

Practice reflection and mindfulness before you fall asleep. An hour before shutting your eye, let the lights go faint within your room. Switch off any electronic gadgets, like your cellphone or TV. Ten minutes before sleep time, start a mindfulness workout. Assuming your mind begins to get sidetracked from your movement or you can perceive that it is meandering, take it back to what you are doing. As you get in bed, focus on your usual relaxation.

- ➢ Be good to yourself and be careful to work on adoring yourself. Get focused on the things you have done that are great. Discuss phrases that mirror the things you wish for yourself.

- ➢ Focus on the way you do your dishes. Be mindful of the bubbles from the cleanser, how it feels against your hands, and how your hands move in the dishwater.

- ➢ Carefully clean your teeth. Focus on how the fibers feel in your mouth and against your teeth. Keep your psyche on each stroke and the flavor of the toothpaste.

- ➢ As you drive down the road, reflect on the way the steering wheel feels. Keep your mind aware of the movement of the vehicle, the manner in which it feels as it goes over the streets, and the shades of the view.

- ➢ Practice with mindfulness. Get to know about how your body feels as you challenge it. Feel the perspiration dribble down your neck and what the burn feels like as you push your body as far as possible.

There is a wide range of ways you can practice mindfulness as you approach your day and the different exercises you tackle.

Significant Stuff to be aware of about Mindfulness

As the definition of mindfulness goes, you are focusing and conscious of your presence. Mindfulness is not an unfamiliar practice or something fanciful; it's an approach to living every day. Mindfulness isn't well specialized in any manner; it is monitoring what your body is doing, what you feel, and what's going on around you each time.

A couple of things you ought to realize about mindfulness are:

> You don't have to change what your identity is or how you appreciate rehearsing mindfulness.

> Mindfulness should be practicable by anybody in any circumstance.

> You might have to really zero in on the thing you are doing as you get everything rolling with mindfulness, yet soon it will end up being a part of you.

- ➢ There is a lot of proof that demonstrates the restorative mental and physical gains of practicing mindfulness.

- ➢ You will actually be able to come up with ingenious thoughts and take care of any other issues by practicing mindfulness.

WHY PRACTICE MINDFULNESS?

There is a great deal of study you can find that urges you to practice mindfulness and how it benefits you. There is denouncing that practicing mindfulness and reflection consistently will be something beneficial for your general prosperity.

Benefits

Mindfulness is really great for your body as it will assist with helping your immune system. A sound immune system will assist with combatting normal diseases so you become ill once in a while and recuperate quicker when you do. Furthermore, since rest is essential to your daily existence, your body will thank you for rehearsing mindfulness each day when you get a better evening's rest.

Practicing mindfulness is additionally really great for your smartness and lucidity. Furthermore, mindfulness lessens pessimistic feelings and psychological well-being issues. Some studies recommend that rehearsing mindfulness in everyday life can assist you with refuting pessimistic sentiments and experiencing more optimistic ones.

Various studies likewise propose that mindfulness can likewise emphatically impact your brain.

❖ **Improve your connections through the normal activities of mindfulness.** Allowing for mindfulness can help your personal and work relationships. By accomplishing a condition of awareness, you will want to zero in on your connections more and come to terms with where the fulfillment comes from. You will be able to communicate your thoughts all the more obviously and manage the pressure that comes with relationship problems.

❖ **Foster a more grounded identity.** You will want to zero in on the things that satisfy you, make you miserable, or irate. You will understand what your triggers are and what you want to stay away from. Rehearsing mindfulness will assist you with having a superior comprehension of yourself and assist you with dealing with dissatisfaction better due to the more certain psychological state.

❖ **When confronted with life-changing circumstances, it tends to be hard to adapt to most people.** Routinely rehearsing mindfulness can assist you with becoming more grounded and adapting better when life tosses you in a tough spot. Mindfulness and brain adaptability go together pleasantly. Together, they can assist you with recuperating from extreme injuries more quickly.

❖ **You can become more dispassionate when confronted with circumstances capable of making you subjective.** The everyday act of mindfulness can assist you with turning out to be less one-sided when confronted with circumstances that call for your settling with a decision. There are testimonies lending credence to the power of mindfulness. Through the ordinary act of mindfulness, you will want to block out interruptions and focus more on what is before you. Thus, you will want to address issues better and settle on well-informed choices.

At long last, through the standard act of mindfulness and reflection, you will be able to cultivate the right empathy within you and develop enviable traits of selflessness.

Who Is Mindfulness Great for?

You don't need to be a yoga devotee or somebody who rehearses a special class to partake in mindfulness.

Mindfulness is perfect for pretty much any individual who needs to have better control of their feelings and ways of behaving. I needed to set the strain of work free from my life and return home to peace.

➢ Traditional mindfulness practice helps business experts to perform various tasks, settle issues, and manage pressure over and above anyone's expectations. I'm a living demonstration of this reality.

➢ Guardians can profit from mindfulness as it will help them with understanding their kids better and serenely handle pressure.

➢ Rehearsing mindfulness can help teens with focusing better and be more mindful. Also, they can deal with the anxieties of teenage life better and with more sympathy.

> ➤ Rehearsing mindfulness in the classroom can help studs. There is reasonable proof that can demonstrate that being mindful in the classroom is exceptionally advantageous to educators and studs.

> ➤ Besides, mindfulness is perfect for inmates in penitentiaries, military veterans, and medical services experts.

Added research has likewise shown that the practice of mindfulness may assist with combatting corpulence.

Simple Reflection and Mindfulness Quick Start Procedures

There are a few basic ways you can begin with mindfulness. There is careful breathing which is a fundamental piece of practicing mindfulness. Another normal practice is the body examination. You focus on each part of your body in turn.

Besides, there are raisin practices where you utilize every one of your faculties consistently. There is additional mediation while you are strolling.

Practice Acceptance

Rehearsing acceptance in mindfulness is perhaps one of the most essential aspects. Acceptance implies assessing your escapades and just recognizing them. Through acknowledgment you don't pass judgment on your experiences as either great or terrible, you simply recognize them for what they are - that they exist. Acceptance demands practice. You may have to attempt it over and over, but no matter what, you can accomplish it.

Weaknesses surrounding Mindfulness

Although the advantages of mindfulness are here present, there are a couple of deficiencies that can show up when you practice mindfulness. But thing is that these inadequacies are uncommon, and the advantages offset them by a long shot. These potential inadequacies are as per the following:

- ➤ Rehearsing care can prompt creating misleading recollections when you focus a lot on something and afterward fill in spaces with made-up information.
- ➤ Some who practice care focus on pessimistic considerations and feelings instead of the good and this can prompt a delicate mental state.
- ➤ Evasion of tough situations can emerge because you are making efforts to become mindful and you confuse that to mean avoiding difficult issues.

In all

Practicing mindfulness in regular daily existence is an extraordinary method for acquiring perspective and getting attuned with your environmental elements, body, mind, and soul. Through careful practice, you can benefit from the varying advantages. Nonetheless, make sure to follow mindfulness and meditation with care and as it should be practiced.

CHAPTER SIX:

PRACTICING HEALTHIER DIETING

In the present dynamic and speed-ridden world, adhering to a sound eating plan is some of the time more difficult than one might expect. The greater part of us knows what it feels like.

First of all, simply filtering through the variety of healthy diets to sort out which one is best for you can be a challenge.

Yet, even after you've selected a dinner plan or consumption pattern, keeping up with that sound eating diet every day of the week can be puzzling

The beautiful news is, regardless of how extreme it could feel a few days, adhering to a solid eating routine is conceivable, and it doesn't imply that you need to surrender your choicest food sources.

There are lots of tips that make eating well simpler, and most of them are basic and free.

The following are 10 of our choicest methods for adhering to a solid eating pattern.

Caveat

"Diet" can mean various things. It can either refer to momentary dietary changes that are normally devoted to weight reduction or another reason (e.g., following the Keto diet), or to an individual's local area's regular approach to eating.

In this chapter, we're zeroing in generally on thoughtful use of diet — a supportable eating pattern that reflects routine food preferences.

1. Eat a diet filled with whole food varieties

There are numerous ways of following a solid eating routine, and no two nutritious weight control plans appear to be identical.

In any case, the best, long-term healthy weight control plans share one thing alike: they are fortified in entire food varieties.

Whole food substances are those that have been barely or even never processed, for example,

- legumes

- vegetables

- Fruits

- Whole grains

- nuts and seeds

- eggs and dairy

- fresh animal proteins

Shakes, enhancements, and craze diets could appear to be helpful on a superficial level, however over time, whole food items have been connected to better health results from one side of the planet to the other.

Whole food sources are high in fiber, nutrients, minerals, and phytonutrients that help a healthy belly and diminish the chances of chronic sicknesses like diabetes and obesity.

Super-processed foods like chips, sweets, and soft drinks are bound to perpetuate irritation and make for constant sicknesses.

Tidbit

Solid weight control plans come in all shapes and sizes, however, a large portion of them are drawn from supplement-based, whole food sources like organic products, vegetables, grains, and protein.

2. Think long and hard before crashing your diet

One of the main questions to ask yourself while beginning a solid eating plan is, "Could I at any point keep this up for the long haul?"

Assuming the solution to that question is no, you could be living on a crash diet.

Crash diets often depend on extreme calorie limitations to get quick weight reduction results

Yet, here's what's about crash diets — really, the thing about consuming fewer calories as a general rule, from Keto to Atkins and everything in-between — the outcomes are not typically rewarding over the long haul. Over the long run, the vast majority of people who diet recover the weight they have lost.

Curiously, one eating regimen that has held up to time is the Mediterranean diet — and it's filled with whole food varieties

Consequently, with regards to staying with a sound diet, make sure to fight the temptation to zero in a lot on weight reduction.

Customarily, the sure propensities you impart by munching a nutritious diet turn out to be more significant over the long haul than how much weight you've lost in a brief timeframe.

Tidbit

Crash dieting from excessive food intake could assist you with getting more fit rapidly, yet that is not beneficial all the time. Besides, there's no assurance the outcomes will endure.

3. Rely on experts to get everything rolling

Basically, taking on a healthy diet can be scary and challenging.

There are such countless weight control plans to look over, that you might feel as if you don't know where to begin. It seems like everybody under the sun has some sort of a test on what you ought to and shouldn't eat.

The good news is you're in good company on this ride.

Many skilled experts can assist you with sorting out the best way for you.

A registered dietitian can assist you with exploring dinner plans, nutrition types, your everyday supplement needs, and safe eating regimens for explicit circumstances and infections.

A behavior change expert, like a clinician, can assist you with getting out of under-old tendencies and creating new ones.

Tidbit

Working with a trained expert is greatly helpful. It similarly guarantees you're getting precise and contemporary information about smart dieting, as well as how to best stay with it.

4. Become familiar with the right eating regimen for you

It's normal to find out about diets depicted as similar to the "best" or "best."

However, nobody's diet turns out best for everybody.

We each live in an exceptional situation impacted by hereditary qualities, our well-being, work plans, family, and social practices, and that's just the beginning.

No single eating routine can impeccably account or oblige for such countless individual variables.

Eventually, the "awesome" proper diet for you is the one that causes you to feel your best and that you can stay with for a long stretch.

Tidbit

Adhering to a solid eating regimen implies finding an approach to eating that isn't just nutritious but also that you see as pleasant, feasible, and helpful for your conditions.

5. Encircle yourself with quality food varieties

Lately, specialists have observed that individuals all over the planet are eating more ultra-processed food varieties than at any time in recent times.

Processed food types are those that have been made by contemporary processing. They will more often than not contain added substances like sugars, thickeners, stabilizers, and different fixings that make the food sources last longer and taste better.

A few instances of ultra-processed food sources include junk food, frozen meals, sugar-filled juices, and soft drinks.

Not exclusively are ultra-processed food varieties enticing because of their flavors, yet in any event, being within the sight of these sorts of food varieties can influence mind science and behavior.

You can help yourself by staying away from the drive to eat these intakes by keeping them out of your home and restricting your access to them at home.

Then again, keeping your cooler and storage space supplied with supplements thick, entire food varieties is an extraordinary method for recalling your sound eating regimen and urging yourself to have those nutritious food sources on a more regular basis.

Tidbit

Keeping yourself with the food varieties you need to eat and figuring out how to cherish them, instead of the ones you're attempting to stay away from, builds your likelihood of getting atop.

6. Continue to fill snacks available

Frequently, it is the time we find out we are hungrier and enticed with a delectable treat that we disregard the smart dieting plans we had as a main priority for the day.

But, longing for certain food substances occasionally is totally welcome, specialists have found that within shots of extreme appetite, our desires will generally get considerably more established.

Keeping nutritious and filling snacks close by is an incredible method for keeping desires under control until your next full dinner.

Bites that are high in protein and fiber can assist with keeping you feeling full.

A few models are:

- fresh leafy fruits and vegetables

- yogurt

- popcorn

- hard-boiled eggs

- blended nuts and nut spreads

- hummus or cooked chickpeas

- entire grain wafers

Tidbit

Staying ready by keeping nutritious and filling snacks available diminishes the possibility of wandering from your sound eating regimen when you are enticed to eat.

7. Relish your favorite food varieties

Have you at any point felt like there's one food you just can't survive without? Luckily, you don't need to!

Denying yourself of the food sources you love and pine for can really end up unhelpful.

In a short while, it will in general make your desires for those food sources much more established, particularly for individuals who are more helpless to food desires as a whole.

Some study has even discovered that feeling content as opposed to being denied while eating less junk food is connected to a higher pace of weight reduction.

Instead of surrendering the less nutritious food varieties that you love, why not consider having them just infrequently while controlling the portions?

Tidbit

The facts confirm that with balance and part control, there is room for all food varieties in a healthy diet — even those that could seem like they could never have some place.

8. Keep away from a 'win-or-die-trying' approach

A typical hindrance individuals experience while making progress toward further developing their weight control plans is falling into a go-hard or go-home mentality.

Such a thought process could sound something like this: "all well and good, I've just hampered my diet for the day by having that piece of cake at the workplace party before, so I can fail to remember my arrangements to cook at home this evening and grab some takeaways instead."

These kinds of considerations as a rule see circumstances clearly, or as "great" and "terrible."

All things considered, attempt to take a gander at every individual food decision you make during a day similar to claim. One not-so-great decision doesn't need to accelerate into an entire day of compromising decisions.

Having high confidence and trust in your capacity to pursue firm decisions will in general be related to better well-being results, so don't allow one little hiccup to cut you down.

Tidbit

Rather than letting the go-hard-or-go-home choices make you imagine that anything short of flawlessness is a disappointment, view each new decision you make about your diet as an utter new plan.

9. Prepare for eating out

For some individuals, potlucks, party time, and feasting out are something to anticipate. However, for somebody striving to adhere to a new or solid eating plan, they can feel like an added hurdle to scale.

Eatery dinners will generally have more calories, sodium, sugar, fat, and ultra-processed food varieties than meals cooked at home, and they frequently come in large servings.

Also, in group settings, our food selections are vigorously impacted by the decisions of individuals around us

Something may get out of hand while eating out, and keeping a sound eating routine while eating out can be somewhat challenging.

In any case, there are ways of making it simpler. Having a plan as a top priority before you get to an eatery or social event can go far in reassuring you and assisting you with feeling ready to deal with eating out.

The following are a couple of hints on eating out:

> Go through the menu before you order.

> Eat a piece of natural produce early.

> Remain hydrated during dinner.

> Request your dinner first.

> Take as much time as necessary and enjoy your dinner.

Tidbit

Preparing for eating out is an extraordinary method for dealing with any pressure or vulnerability you could feel about how you'll adhere to your healthy diet at an eatery or some event.

10. Keep an eye on your Progress

Being observant is a simple and compelling method for monitoring your advancement all alone

It very well may be simple as straightforward as keeping a diary of the food varieties you eat every day or as definite as using a cellphone or some virtual app that tracks the details of your day-to-day calorie consumption, weight, movement levels, and the sky is the limit from there.

While self-checking your progress, always recollect that weight gain and reduction are by all accounts not the only ways of estimating how far you've come. At times, they probably won't be the most effective way to quantify progress all things considered.

Individuals decide to follow sound weight control plans for a wide range of different reasons. For instance, you could decide to zero in on what your dietary changes have meant for your physical or psychological well-being, as opposed to how much weight you've lost.

A few different inquiries to pose to yourself to assist with estimating whether your selected eating program is working are:

- Am I full and fulfilled?

- Do I appreciate what I eat?

- Might I at some point continue to eat this way until the end of time?

- What number of solid decisions did I make today?

- How sure do I feel about my eating routine?

- Have I seen any progressions in my actual well-being?

Have I seen any progressions in my psychological wellness?

Tidbit

Assess your advancement to evaluate whether your endeavors are having their planned outcomes. Be that as it may, following doesn't need to mean logging each calorie on an app! Checking in with your body can be sufficient to assist you with adhering to a nutritious diet.

Endeavor to show restraint toward yourself. Adhering to a better eating routine is a long-distance race, not just a run.

Learning the best eating routine for yourself takes experimentation, and every day will be simpler than others, so make an effort not to feel deterred assuming it takes more time than you'd like for your new lifestyle to set in.

However long you set reasonable assumptions for yourself, stay committed, and keep on rethinking your progress, your eating regimen is probably going to continue to move in a positive bearing.

Tidbit

Developing new habits of any sort demands time, and healthy dieting as well. While you're feeling baffled, consider practicing self-consciousness and pulling together your drawn-out objectives.

For all it is worth

Bringing an end to habits and developing new ones is not a simple process, particularly with regards to food varieties you've been eating for what seems like forever.

Our diets are complicated systems impacted by natural, mental, and social impacts, just to give some examples

Hence, different approaches might be expected to explore those elements and adhere to a sound eating routine in the long run.

CHAPTER SEVEN:

TAKING IT BACK: LESS STRESS, FOCUSED SPEED

I understood that to improve on my focus, it was insufficient just to weed out interruptions. That encourages you from the start - however, at that point, it makes a vacuum where the entire craving was. I understood I should fill the vacuum. That's what to do; I began to contemplate an area of psychological research I had found out about years prior - the study of stream currents. Nearly everybody perusing this will have encountered a stream current sometimes back. It refers to the point, at which you are doing something significant to you, and you truly get into it, and time falls away, and your self-image appears to disappear, and you end up focusing profoundly and easily. Stream is the most profound type of focus that people can offer. In any case, how would we achieve this?

I later consulted Dr. Lindelof Fall in Lund, Sweden, who was one of the principal researchers to study stream currents and explored them for over 25 years. From his examination, I realized there are three key elements that you want to get into the stream. First, you want to pick one objective. Stream takes generally your psychological energy, conveyed purposely in one course. Second, that objective should be significant to you - you can't stream into an objective that you couldn't care less about. Third, it helps to assume what you are doing is at the edge of your capacities - if, say, the stone you are climbing is marginally higher and harder than the last stone you climbed. So each day, I began to compose - an alternate sort of composition from my prior work, one that surpassed me. In a couple of days, I began to stream, and long stretches of the center would pass without it seeming like a test. I believed I was focusing on the manner I had when I was a young person, in lengthy easy stretches. I had dreaded my mind breaking. I cried with alleviation when I figured out that in the right conditions, its full power could return.

Toward the finish of every day, I would sit on the ocean front and watch the light leisurely change. The light on the cape is not normal for the light elsewhere I have at any point been and in Connecticut, I could see more plainly than I at any point had before in my life - my contemplation, my own objectives, my fantasies. I was living in the light. So when the opportunity arrived to take off from the ocean side house and return to the hyperlinked world, I became persuaded I had deciphered the code of focus. I got back to still up in the air to apply the points I had learned in my regular daily existence. At the point when I got back to my cellphone and PC after returning a ship to where they were reserved in Miami, they appeared to be unfamiliar and estranging. Yet, in a couple of months, my screen time had returned to four hours every day, and my consideration was fraying and breaking once more.

Having a heart-to-heart talk with Martin Gary of Completeness Worldview in Dublin one night, I may as yet review his words about people returning to themselves. Martin commented that singular restraint is "not the arrangement, for the very reason that wearing a gas veil for four days in fourteen outside isn't the response to contamination. It may, for a brief timeframe, keep specific impacts under control, however, it's not practical, and it doesn't resolve the fundamental issues." He said that our attention is profoundly changed by enormous obtrusive powers in a more extensive society. Saying the arrangement was to simply change your propensities - to promise to part ways with your telephone, say - was "pushing it back on to the person" he said, when "actually the natural changes will truly have the effect".

Martin noted it could assist me with getting a grip on what's going on if we contrast our increasing focus issues with our increasing heftiness rates. Quite a while back there were little to no weight gain issues, yet today it is endemic in the Western world. This isn't because we unexpectedly became voracious or narcissistic. He said: "Overweight is certainly not a clinical plague - it's a social pestilence. We have terrible food, for instance, thus individuals are getting fat." How we live changed emphatically - our food supply changed, and we fabricated urban communities that are difficult to walk or cycle around, and those adjustments to our current circumstance prompted changes in our bodies.

I discovered that the elements hurting our attention are not all promptly self-evident. I had been consumed by tech without abeyance, however as a matter of fact the causes range broadly - from the food we eat to the air we inhale, from the hours we work to the hours we never again rest. They consist of numerous things we have come to underestimate - from how we deny our children of play, to how our schools strip learning of importance by putting together all that concerning tests. I came to accept we want to answer this unending intrusion of our focus at two levels. The first is the person. There is a wide range of changes we can make at an individual level that will safeguard our concentration. I would agree that by doing the greater part of them, I have supported my concentration by around 18%. In any case, we need to even out with individuals. Those changes will just take you up to this point. Right now, it's like we are having tingling powder poured over us the entire day, and individuals pouring the powder are saying: "You should figure out how to meditate. Then you wouldn't need to scratch so badly a lot." Reflection is a helpful instrument - however, we really need to stop individuals who are pouring tingling powder on us. We want to come together as one grasping our focus and taking it back.

CHAPTER EIGHT:

IN CHARGE OF THE PACE: MUSIC AND READING

Many individuals discover that music helps them with focusing while at the same time meditating and working. Others find it hard to concentrate with any foundation trouble whatsoever.

Music offers a ton of advantages, including:

- further developed temperament

- expanded inspiration

- support focus

- further developed memory and brain excitement

- better administration of agony and weariness

Yet, not every person concurs that music further develops a review meeting. So what's going on — does it help or not?

Music doesn't influence everybody similarly, so the response isn't simply a clear "yes" or "no."

Continue to peruse to dive deeper into the upsides and downsides of examining music and get a few ways to make the most out of your review playlist.

How it can help

Hopefully, you will put on a playlist or tune that could end up being useful to you in taking out an issue set or remembering the many dates for your set of experiences last.

But, music isn't exactly strong. It generally helps in indirect ways; however, those advantages can in any case have a major effect.

It diminishes pressure and works on your state of mind

Music doesn't simply rouse you. It can likewise assist with lessening pressure and advancing a more sure mentality.

In a 2021 study, 70 male workers did a mental pressure test while paying attention to loosening up music, hints of undulating water, or no specific sound. Results recommended that attending to liberating music has an actual effect on how individuals react mentally and— concerning chemical reactions — under pressure. Notwithstanding, the image is intricate, and more examinations are required.

In a 2022 assessment, patients in ICU said they felt less agony and nervousness in the wake of paying attention to music for 20 minutes than previously.

Research recommends that a positive state of mind by and large further develops your learning results. You'll probably have more accomplishments with examining and learning new material while you're feeling better.

Reading can be distressing, particularly when you don't figure out the subject material. If you feel overpowered or upset, putting on some music can help you unwind and work all the more successfully.

It can push you

If you've at any point wrestled with a long, debilitating evening of schoolwork, your purpose to continue to review might have begun to signal well before you wrapped up.

Maybe you guaranteed yourself compensation to traverse the review meeting, for example, the most recent episode of a show you like or your number one takeout dinner.

Research from 2020 recommends music can actuate similar prize places in your cerebrum as different things you appreciate. Compensating yourself with your #1 music can give the inspiration you want to learn new data.

In case you lean toward music that doesn't admirably suit you building your attention to your main tunes during the focus on breaks could rouse you to study harder.

It can cement your focus

As indicated by a recent report, music — traditional music, explicitly — can help your brain absorb and decipher new data all the more without any problem.

Your mind processes the overflow of information it gets from your general surroundings by isolating it into more modest sections.

The scientists tracked down evidence to recommend that music can draw in your mind so that it trains it to focus harder on occasions and make expectations about what could occur.

How does this assist you with meditating? Indeed, if you battle to figure out new material, paying attention to music could make this interaction more straightforward.

You can likewise interface the capacity to improve expectations about events to thinking abilities.

Further developed capabilities to think won't assist you with hauling responses out of nowhere when tested. Be that as it may, you could perceive a distinction in your capacity to think about your direction to these responses because of the information you do have.

Other research likewise upholds music as a potential strategy for further developing attention.

In a 2021 wellness study of 54 young men established to have ADHD, ambient sound diverted a portion of the young men; however, it seemed to prompt better execution in the homeroom for other people.

It could assist you with retaining information

As per 2021 research, paying attention to traditional music appeared to assist more seasoned grown-ups with performing better on memory and processing activities.

These discoveries propose particular sorts of music can assist with supporting retention capacities and other mental capabilities.

Music invigorates your cerebrum, like how exercise animates your body.

Is it not the case that the more you stretch your muscles, the more grounded they become? Giving your brain a mental exercise could assist with reinforcing it likewise.

How it can be unhelpful

Not every person finds music accommodating for activities that require focus.

You can get distracted

A significant part of music's effects lies in its capability to distract.

At the point when you feel miserable or pushed, diverting yourself with your #1 tune can assist with cheering you up.

Be that as it may, interruption most likely isn't the thing you're searching for when you want to raise a ruckus around town.

If you're attempting to test a thesis about your situation in a research project or settle a troublesome math condition, music that is too clear or quick may very well interfere with your thought processes and obstruct your cycle.

It can adversely affect working memory

Working memory refers to the information you use for critical thinking, learning, and other mental assignments.

You utilize working memory while attempting to recollect:

- things on a rundown

- ventures for taking care of a numerical question

- a grouping of occasions

The vast majority can work with a couple of snippets of data all at once. A high working memory limit implies you can deal with more material.

The research proposes, notwithstanding, that standing by listening to music can diminish working memory limit.

Assuming that, as of now, you struggle with controlling numerous snippets of data, understand that paying attention to music could make this cycle much more seriously challenging.

It can bring down empathetic perception

Specific kinds of music — incorporating music with verses and instrumental music that is quick and uproarious — can make it harder to comprehend and retain understanding material.

Whether you're taking a gander at a night of Victorian writing or somebody on-one time with your science course reading, delicate traditional music with a steady rhythm might be a superior decision.

What sort of music works best?

Paying attention to music while you study or work doesn't necessarily make you less useful or less proficient. Remembering these tips can assist you with tracking down the most suitable music for work and study:

- **Keep away from music with verses**. Any music that has verses in a language you comprehend will likely prove more distracting than supportive.

- **Pick slow, instrumental music**. Existing research for the most part centers on traditional music, yet if you despise this sort, you could likewise consider delicate and benevolent ones you could hear at a spa or while getting a back rub.

- **Abstain from astonishing or trial music.** Music that changes unexpectedly or comes up short on fixed mood can leave you speculating about what's in store. This can divert your mind and hold you back from zeroing in on your work.

- **Keep the volume low**. Concentrating on music while studying or working ought to be kept at a low volume. If it's excessively loud, it could upset your reasoning interaction.

- **Stick to melodies you don't have unmistakable dispositions toward.** Paying attention to the music you either love or disdain can influence your capacity to think.

- **If practicable, try to stream business-free music**. Picture this: You're standing by listening to your instrumental

Pandora station when an airline ad cuts in, irritating you and disrupting your line of reasoning.

CHAPTER NINE:

SELF-CARE IT IS: ROSES CAN STAY UNRUFFLED

The capacity to experience and communicate feelings is more expedient than you could understand.

As the felt reaction to a given circumstance, feelings have a critical impact on your responses. At the point when you're on top of them, you approach significant information that assists with:

- navigation

- relationship achievement

- everyday relationships

- taking care of oneself

While feelings can play a supportive part in your routine, they can negatively affect your emotional wellbeing and relational connections when you begin to feel wild.

Canister Martin, a specialist in Stockholm, Sweden, makes it clear that any emotion — even delight, euphoria, or others you'd regularly consider to be positive — can get so much to where it becomes hard to control.

With some regular practice, however, you can reclaim the rules. Two examinations from a 2021 study propose that having great emotional abilities is linked to doing well. Besides, the next study tracked down a possible connection between these abilities and monetary achievement, such that investing some energy on that front may in a real sense pay off.

Here are a few pointers to help you thrive.

1. Assess the effect of your feelings

Serious feelings aren't all awful.

"Feelings make our lives invigorating, special, and energetic," Canister says. "Overwhelming leanings can imply that we embrace life completely, that we're not quelling our regular responses."

It's entirely commonplace to encounter some profound overwhelm now and again — when something magnificent occurs when something horrendous occurs when you feel like you've passed up a major opportunity.

All in all, how do you have any idea when there's an issue?

Feelings that consistently go crazy could prompt:

- Friendship or relationship struggle

- trouble connecting with others

- an inconvenience at work or school

- an inclination to utilize substances to assist with dealing with your feelings

- physical or emotional eruptions

Make out an opportunity to consider exactly how your uncontrolled feelings impact your everyday life. This will make it more straightforward to recognize trouble spots (and follow up on your success).

2. Go for balance, not constraint

You have no control over your feelings with a dial (if by some stroke of good luck it were that simple!). However, envision, briefly, that you could deal with feelings along these lines.

You would have zero desire to leave them running at the most extreme constantly. You additionally would have no desire to turn them off completely, by the same token.

At the point when you stifle or quell feelings, you're keeping yourself from encountering and communicating feelings. This can happen intentionally (concealment) or unknowingly (suppression).

Either can add to mental and actual health side effects, including:

- uneasiness

- despondency

- rest issues

- muscle pressure and torment

- trouble managing pressure

- substance abuse

While figuring out how to manage feelings, ensure you're not simply hiding them where no one will think to look. A solid profound idea includes discovering little unity between overpowering feelings and no feelings by any means.

3. Distinguish what you feel

Pausing for a minute to check in with yourself about your mindset can assist you with restoring control.

Let's assume you've been seeing somebody for a couple of months. You took a stab at arranging a date last week; however, they said they don't have the time and energy. Once more, recently, you messaged, saying, "I might want to see you soon. Could you at any point meet this week?" They at last answer, over a day after the fact: "Can't. I've got so much on my plate."

You become so incredibly disturbed. Without ceasing to think, you fling your cellphone across the room, push over your wastebasket, and kick your workspace objects, hitting your toe.

Ask yourself:

What do I feel at present? (Frustrated, befuddled, enraged)

What occurred to make me feel such? (They forgot about me for no great reason.)

Does what is going on have a different clarification that could seem OK? (Perhaps they're anxious, debilitated, or managing something different they feel awkward explaining. They could want to make sense of more when they can.)

What is it that I believe should work for these sentiments? (Shout; vent my disappointment by tossing things, text back something discourteous.)

Is there a superior approach to adapting to them? (Inquire as to whether all is great. Ask when they're free right on. Take a walk or run.)

By taking into account potential other options, you're reexamining your contemplations, which can assist you with adjusting your initial flash-in-the-pan response.

It can take some amount of time before this reaction turns into a tendency. With practice, going through these approaches in your mind will become simpler (and more powerful).

4. Acknowledge your feelings — every one of them

Since you're attempting to get better at dealing with feelings, you could make efforts towards mirroring your emotions towards yourself.

At the point when you hyperventilate on hearing some good news or break down on the floor shouting and crying when you can't wrap your head around something, it seems helpful to tell yourself,

"Simply quiet down," or "It isn't so large of an arrangement, so don't go crazy."

Yet, this refutes your experience. It is nothing to joke about for you.

Tolerating feelings in real terms is helpful to you in becoming more aware of them. Expanding your solace around intense feelings lets you completely feel them without responding in outrageous, pointless ways.

To work on tolerating feelings, try to approach them as message carriers. They're unbiased. Perhaps they are horrendous feelings some of the time, however, they're giving you significant information that you can make do with.

For instance, attempt to say:

"I'm disturbed since I cope with this, which makes me late. I ought to put a dish on the rack by the entryway so I make sure to leave them in a similar spot."

Accepting your feelings might prompt more significant life fulfillment and provoke fewer psychological health side effects. In addition, individuals considering their feelings as accommodating may provoke more elevated levels of satisfaction.

5. Keep a temperament diary

Putting on paper (or composing) your feelings and the reactions they trigger can assist you with revealing any problematic examples.

Now and again, it's okay to follow emotions back through your intellectual thoughts. Registering how you feel on paper can help you to profoundly consider them better.

It also helps you with perceiving when explicit conditions, like an inconvenience at work or a family struggle, contribute to more difficult feelings. Recognizing explicit triggers makes it conceivable to think of ways of managing them all the more gainfully.

Journaling offers the most advantage when you do it day to day. Keep your diary with you and scribble down deep feelings or emotions as they occur. Attempt to take note of the triggers and your response. If your response didn't help, leverage your diary to look into more suitable opportunities for what's in store.

6. Take a full breath

There's a lot to be said for the force of a full breath, whether you're strangely blissful or so furious you can't talk.

Slowing down and focusing on your breath won't make the feelings disappear (and recollect, that is not the objective).

In any case, profound breathing activities can assist you with establishing yourself and make a stride back from the intense feelings and any outrageous responses you need to keep away from.

The subsequent time you feel emotions are beginning to take their toll:

❖ Take a breath leisurely. Full breaths come from the stomach, not the chest. It might assist with envisioning your breath ascending from somewhere down in your tummy.

❖ Hold on to it. Pause your breathing for a count of three, then, at that point, let it out steadily.

❖ Think about a mantra. Certain individuals find it supportive to follow a mantra, similar to "I'm quiet" or "I'm free."

7. Know when to put yourself out there

There's an appropriate setting for everything, including serious feelings. Wailing wildly is a typical reaction to losing a friend or family member, for instance. Screaming hard into your cushion, in any event, punching it could assist you with easing a few resentment and pressure should you feel dumped.

Different circumstances, notwithstanding, require some limitations. Regardless of how baffled you are, shouting at your supervisor over an 'uncalled-for' disciplinary activity won't help.

Being aware of your environmental elements and the circumstance can assist you in understanding when it's alright to express yourself and when you should sit with them for the time being.

8. Give yourself some space

Getting some separation from serious feelings can assist you with ensuring you're responding to them in sensible ways, as per Canister.

This distance may be physical, such as leaving what is happening, for instance. In any case, you can likewise make some psychological distance by diverting yourself.

While you would rather not block or stay away from feelings completely, it's not hurtful to occupy yourself until you're in a superior place to manage them. Simply get back in the saddle to them. Some interruptions are short-term.

Attempt:

- going for a stroll

- watching an interesting video

- conversing with a friend or family member

- Making up a few minutes with your pet

9. Choose to meditate

That's what it is – a choice. Amid the hustle and bustle of metropolitan life, the art of meditation has essentially become a choice to be made. If you practice reflection as we speak, it very well may be one of your go-to strategies for adapting to extreme feelings.

Meditation can assist you with expanding your consciousness of all feelings and experiences. At the point when you think, you're training yourself to sit with those thoughts, to see them without passing judgment on yourself or endeavoring to change them or make them disappear.

As said above, figuring out how to acknowledge every one of your feelings can make emotional balance easier to come by. Reflection assists you with expanding those appreciative abilities. It also offers different advantages, such as helping you unwind and get better rest.

Our manual for various sorts of reflection can assist you with getting everything rolling.

10. Keep steady under overpressure

At the point when you're under a whole bulk of stress, dealing with your feelings can turn out to be more worrisome. Indeed, even individuals who by and large have some control over their feelings well could track down it harder amid high pressure and stress.

Stress reduction, or following up on supportive ways of overseeing it, can help your feelings with becoming more sensible.

Mindfulness practices such as reflection can help in managing stress, as well. Such practices will not dispose of it, yet they can make stress simpler to live with.

Other solid ways of adapting to pressure include:

- getting sufficient rest

- creating time to talk and laugh with loved ones

- working out

- staying close to nature

- setting aside some time for relaxation and other side interests.